MY SISTER — LIFE

MY SISTER – LIFE

Boris Pasternak

Translated from the Russian by Mark Rudman

WITH BOHDAN BOYCHUK

NORTHWESTERN UNIVERSITY PRESS

EVANSTON, ILLINOIS

Northwestern University Press
Evanston, Illinois 60208-4210

Printed in the United States of America

10 9 8 7 6 5 4 3 2 1

ISBN 0-8101-1909-9

Library of Congress Cataloging-in-Publication Data

Pasternak, Boris Leonidovich, 1890–1960
    [Sestra moia zhizn'. English]
    My sister—life / Boris Pasternak ; translated by
Mark Rudman with Bohdan Boychuk.
        p. cm. — (European Poetry Classics)
        ISBN 0-8101-1909-9 (pbk. : alk. paper)
        I. Rudman, Mark. II. Boichuk, Bohdan. III. Title. IV.
    Series.

    PG3476.P27 S413 2001
    891.71'42—dc21

                                            2001034544

DEDICATED TO LERMONTOV

CONTENTS

PREFACE / *Mark Rudman*

Boris Pasternak in entire purity of heart, surrounding himself with all his materials, writes, copies from life—right down to its inadvertencies! ... The main character in his work is—trees at a meeting. Over Pasternak's Square it is *they* that are the ringleaders. Whatever Pasternak might write, it is always the elements, not the characters. *Marina Tsvetaeva*

THIS BOOK is the result of a collaboration that has taken place intermittently over a six year period with Bohdan Boychuk, the Ukrainian poet. We first met in 1972 while working on another translation project (Ivan Drach's selected poems, *Orchard Lamps*). After the sessions we would talk about Russian poetry that I had only read in translation. I was particularly curious about Pasternak's *My Sister—Life*, since every mention of it by Russian poets and critics was tinged with awe and excitement. It was clear from reviews and commentaries by his contemporaries that *My Sister—Life* was considered a seminal book in Russian poetry. Osip Mandelstam said at the time, "To read the poems of Pasternak is to get one's throat clear, to fortify one's breathing ... I see Pasternak's *My Sister—Life* as a collection of magnificent exercises in breathing ... a cure for tuberculosis." Marina Tsvetaeva reacted in kind: "*My Sister—Life!* The first thing I did, when I'd borne it all, from the first blow to the last, was spread my arms out wide, so that the joints all cracked. I was caught in it, as in a downpour ... a downpour of light."

But the existing translations—particularly of the early, ground-breaking poetry—conveyed none of this wonder to me, to my American ear. When I asked what made Pasternak's work so compelling, Boychuk's face would light up, he would become suddenly animated and alert. He made it clear that there was no way to *explain*. It became apparent that the only way I was going to get to know Pasternak's early poetry was to translate it. There began our collaboration. And here is the result.

—

We took on this Quixotic project as a challenge. It appealed to the problem-solving side of our natures, since the more we worked, the more apparent it became that any solution was only a "momentary stay against confusion." In many ways it has been an ongoing dialogue between three poets, three cultures, and three languages. There was an intense tug of war between the Russian and English. Neither Boychuk nor I wanted to compromise in terms of language. If I came up with what I thought was an inspired line, Boychuk would have none of it if he felt it violated Pasternak's deepest intention in any way. When unable to convey the gist of a given image through words, Boychuk would sometimes get up and mime the action implied in/by/through the language, to express, for example, just how softly and quietly "the rain shuffled" from foot to foot in the poem "There Were."

It took us about three years to get a working version of the original text. To give some idea of the process: Boychuk would read me the poem in Russian to give me a sense of its rhythm; then he would reread each stanza and dictate it word for word in English, keeping the Russian syntax and describing its formal components. Afterward I would do a rough version and send it to him with a list of questions. It was only after this that our equivalent of a literal version would evolve.

In the meantime I read everything I could lay my hands on—all extant translations of the poetry and the criticism. Pasternak was fortunate in his Russian critics (Abram Lezhnev, Yury Tynyanov, Wladimir Weidle, to name a few) who went to great lengths to understand his poetry before judging it. One of the things that was most helpful and cleared up certain lingering doubts and points of confusion was to find that these critics found the poems in *My Sister—Life* ranged from the complex to what Lezhnev calls "deliberate" unintelligibility. Pasternak's early poetry turned out to be much stranger, and in the case of "The Highest Sickness" more maniacal, than either Boychuk or I had anticipated from the first reading.

Pasternak, when he wrote *My Sister—Life*, was enchanted. To comprehend this we need to look anew at him. At what defined the young Pasternak, not what defined the narrator of *Doctor Zhivago* or the image imprinted on his character and perpetuated by the intensely somber photographs. In these he appears to be anything but the defiant, innovative young poet, writing dense, oblique poetry. Pasternak, who conceived of art as a sponge, thought it would be impossible for anyone to write authentic lyric poetry except in what he called "intermittent bursts of inspiration." His poetry is wild *and* controlled.

> In the orphaned, sleepless,
> damp universal waste,
> groans tore from their posts,
> the whirlwind dug in, abated.
> ("A SULTRY NIGHT")

Even in "The Highest Sickness," one of the most personal, social-political poems ever written, Pasternak does not relinquish his lyricism in the service of an epic theme—the revolutionary epoch.

> Although the dawn thistle
> kept on chasing its shadow
> and in the same motion
> made the hour linger;
> although, as before, the dirt road
> dragged the wheels over soft white sand
> and spun them onto harder ground
> alongside signs and landmarks;
> although the autumn sky was cloudy,
> and the forest appeared distant,
> and the twilight was cold and hazy,
> anyway, it was all a forgery.

And the sleep of the stunned earth
was convulsive, like labor pains,
like death, like the silence
of cemeteries, like that unique quiet
that blankets the horizon,
shudders, and beats its brains
to remember: Hold on, prompt me,
what did I want to say?

Andrei Sinyavsky, in his Introduction to the Soviet edition of Pasternak's collected poetry, locates the essential trajectory of the poem: "pictures of revolution, war and destruction, not set out in the form of a consecutive narrative, but as if dissolved in the involuntary flow of the verse." "Involuntary" is the key word here. Evidently this is the way Pasternak's mind worked, the way he spoke. Isaiah Berlin observed:

He spoke in magnificent slow-moving periods, with occasional intense rushes of words. His talk often overflowed the banks of grammatical structure—lucid passages were succeeded by wild but always marvelously vivid and concrete images—and these might be followed by dark words when it was difficult to follow him—and then he would suddenly come into the clear again. His speech was at all times that of a poet, as were his writings.

And in "The Highest Sickness" instead of telling a story or availing himself of narrative techniques, Pasternak gives us an extended digression, a kaleidoscopic view of the age, culminating in a double-edged portrait of Lenin.

—

The fifty poems in *My Sister—Life* form a continuous sequence structured around arrivals and departures, train rides to and from the city and the poet's summer dacha, and centers around several relationships between the "I" and the "other," the poet and his loves. According to Sinyavsky, its appearance marked Pasternak as "one of the masters of contemporary verse."

My Sister—Life was published in 1922, but in fact it was written during the summer of 1917, in the months before the October Revolution. And although the Revolution is only mentioned directly in a few of the poems, it permeates the book—as energy, a sense of beginning again. Later on Pasternak expressed his sense of it in this way: "I saw upon earth a summer that seemed not to recognize itself—natural, prehistoric, as in a revelation. I left a book about it. In that book I expressed everything that can possibly be learnt of the most improbable, the most elusive things about the Revolution."

> In whose heart does the blood rush
> toward glory pouring down drawn cheeks?
> There the blood beats: the prime minister's hands
> strangle aortas and mouths.
>
> It's not the night, not rain, nor the chorus
> erupting: "Kerensky, hooray!"
> It's a blinding exit to the Forum
> from catacombs, that yesterday had no way out.
>
> It's not roses, not mouths, nor the roar
> of multitudes thronging at the gates—
> but the tide of Europe's night
> swelling with pride on our pavements.
> ("SPRING RAINSTORM")

—

Boris Leonidovich Pasternak was born on February 10 (January 29) 1890, in Moscow. His father was the well-known artist Leonid Pasternak, his mother the pianist Rosa Kaufman. The poet's childhood years were spent in an atmosphere of art, music and literature. The many-sided cultural interests and connections of his family were reflected very early in his inclinations. Thus, while he was still a child or young boy, an indelible impression was made on him by the German poet Rilke, by Leo Tolstoy and by Scriabin. He has spoken of these first encounters with artistic genius as having been of definitive importance for the formation of his own cast of mind. *Andrei Sinyavsky*

The effect that Tolstoy, Scriabin, and Rilke had on Pasternak during childhood allowed Pasternak to take for granted what the "age" would come to question: the necessity of art. He was one of the least "alienated" of twentieth century poets.

Pasternak's poetry reflects a synthesis of musical, painterly, and novelistic elements and techniques. His poems combine sound, image and narative, all linked together by the specificity of objects. This he may have learned from Rilke. But unlike Rilke, who in *New Poems* honed in on isolated objects and whose poems such as "The Panther" or "Archaic Torso of Apollo," evolved out of extended concentration on them, Pasternak was more attentive to the flow, the constant movement and change that occurs from moment to moment and in the hitherto unseen connection between disparate things.

> But the sky, under the banners
> of mumbling clouds,
> did not hear my prayer
> through the heavy silence,
> sodden, like an army overcoat,
> like the dusty sound of threshing,
> like a noisome squabble in the bushes.
> I pleaded with them—
> don't torture me!
> I can't sleep!
>
> But it went on drizzling,
> and clouds kept crossing the dusty market
> like recruits filing past a farmhouse at dawn,
> not for an hour, not for a century,
> like Austrian prisoners of war,
> like a muffled gasp,
> like a hoarse cry:
> "Sister ...
> some ... water. ..."
> ("AN EVEN MORE SULTRY DAWN")

Pasternak has a radically original way of looking at the world—as though it were born again every day. There is nothing he does not marvel at. The simplest act is miracle to him. "In our wooden dacha/anything could happen." He never unlearned spontaneity and the fact that her saw no contradiction between being playful and being serious left him free to respond to dailiness with primordial force.

> Summer waved goodbye to the wayside
> station. Then thunder
> took off its cap and snapped
> a hundred blinding photographs.
>
> A lilac cluster dimmed and
> thunder gathered sheaves
> of lightning to expose, from far
> fields, the overseer's house.
> ("STORM, AND ENDLESS INSTANT")

Pasternak is continually astonished to discover that he exists in the midst of so much flux, for nothing in his poetry is stationary, everything quivers, on the verge of motion; the very "air of the steppe is alerted," in rain every leaf longs to "surge toward the steppe," "train doors scatter over the endless plain."

Pasternak is as unselfconscious as he is sophisticated. Even in the group of poems in the section "Lectures on Philosophy" that focus on the role of art and the artist, Pasternak puts philosophical concepts by the board. He uses the titles to create a certain expectation in the reader which he then upends. What is poetry in "The Definition of Poetry"?

> It's a tightly filled whistle,
> it's the squeaking of jostled ice,
> it's night, frosting the leaves,
> it's two nightingales dueling.

Pasternak conveys ideas through sense perceptions and in the process sets up a dialogue between logic and intuition. In a way these poems could be read as a legacy of the younger Pasternak who, still in search of a vocation, made his pilgrimage to the University of Marburg to study philosophy with the esteemed professor Hermann Cohen.

Czeslaw Milosz perceived that Pasternak "did not pluck fruits from the tree of reason, the tree of life was enough for him. Confronted by argument, he replied with his sacred dance. ... Pasternak's poetry is antispeculative, anti-intellectual ... His worship of life meant a fascination with what can be called nature's moods—air, rain, clouds, snow in the streets, a detail changing thanks to the time of the day or night, to the season."

The seasons, the "you" or lover, sounds, the landscape, the heat and the cold, eyes, disease—these give the book its form. It's the repetition and admixture of any or all of these ingredients in each individual poem and in the relation of one poem to another that gives *My Sister—Life* unity; it's the way he introduces a new subject, theme or metaphor in the middle of a poem, like "the year" in "Mein Liebchen, was willst du noch mehr?" that

> guttered in kereosene
> like a gnat trapped in a lamp,
> then got up, a gray-blue star,
> sleepy and wet.

"The year" gives the poem a microscopic, intense focus—it enters as another being with a character of its own, "a gnat trapped in a lamp."

—

The strangeness of these poems comes from the onrush of loosely linked perceptions, from the angle of vision, the perspective or context in which they're placed, from the combination of linear and associative techniques.

It was shadows taking your pulse; it was you
turning your face toward the fields
that burned, swimming on the hinges of gates
flooded with dusk, ashes and poppies.

It was the whole summer in a blaze of pods
and labels and sun-bleached luggage
sealing the wanderer's breast with wax,
setting your hats and dresses on fire.
("POSTSCRIPT")

The quality of attention to detail makes the poem timebound,
contingent. In *My Sister—Life* most of the poems are located in very
specific places—the train station, the Moochkap teahouse—objects
and nature enact the drama. Pasternak is convinced that objects,
sequestered and changed by imagination, are sacred and that the
bond between the perceiver and the thing perceived is an index of
the value of an encounter between the self and the world.

"The Flies of the Moochkap Teahouse" illustrates Pasternak's
approach and is paradigmatic of his method. Like so many of the
poems in *My Sister—Life* it has a triadic structure: departure,
encounter, return. The poem begins with a direct address to "you,"
a lover who has rejected him again; her angry gaze has thrown him
into a fit, into a stae of heightened consciousness in the teahouse
"where black cherries/peer out of eye sockets" and "black tea floods
the room/in the heat of transgression."

The other subject of the poem—heat and the accompanying
effects—emerges when:

an oak, enameled billboards,
sun-crazed, collapse
and hurl themselves
into the jaspered pond.

guise of heat Pasternak projects his own feelings of anger, and rejection onto the objects in the teahouse, onto ak, the enameled billboards. He narrates the events as though they were actually happening in nature, outside the poem, and yet this "action" takes place in the mirror of the pond; reflections, like imagination, multiply and distort.

Only after this do the "flies," the triggering subject of the poem, appear; Pasternak merges the inside (teahouse) and the outside (pond):

> But even after dark, flies flow
> by the dozen from steaming portions
> from the "twisted lord"
> and the poet's muddy book.

The poem opens up here and begins to whirl. Pasternak works through an initially negative and painful emotion and state of intense tension ("The sun's like blood on a knife,/washed—it gives off a strange glow") into an ecstatic release: "It's as though some delirious pen/had squirted out of control," like "locusts." And the "whirring spiral of storm" looks exactly like, has grown out of, emerged from the flies buzzing around, flowing "by the dozen from steaming portions."

> It's as though the time had come
> for all springs to leap from their hinges,
> for the whirring spiral of storm
> to spin around the poplar.

The poem ends on a calmer tone, the moment before a storm. And once again this ending on the weather connects the feeling of something about to burst internally with something about to burst externally.

But where, in what place,
in what country of wild thoughts?
I know drought and thunder, and when
a storm will break in July—I know.

—

My primary concern with each poem was that it exist as a verbal object according to the laws of its own nature, independent of and entirely dependent upon the original text. I tried to draw the English poems from the landscape and dramatic situation, to reimagine them, to visualize them in my imagination, to body them forth through their psychic as well as physical space, their overall reverberation, their subtext, their undertone. The real translation took place away from the text in the same way that silence precedes true speech. It is as much a sensual as an intellectual process.

MOOCHKAP

The spirit sweats—the horizon's
tobacco-tinged—like thought.
Windmills image a fishing village:
boats and weathered nets.

The village of torpid windmills
hovers like a motionless harbor.
All smells of weary stasis,
uneasiness, and grief.

The hours skip past like stones,
richochet across the shallows,
not drowning, keeping afloat,
tobacco-tinged—like thought.

There's time before the train
but it's drowned by apathy,
sunk in limbo, the roiling
turbulence before a storm.

I wanted to convey the tactile quality of the sensations embodied in the language, not only to recreate the phenomenally dense imagery, but also to capture the rapid diction, and associative texture of Pasternak's narrative.

But I hardly knew where to begin, that is, how to get everything within the ubiquitous quatrain, create and maintain momentum that would carry headlong through the concatenation of images to the end. I had no model or precedent for the kind of form I thought these poems demanded except perhaps Basil Bunting's *Briggflats* for its welding of sound and image and thing ("A mason times his mallet/to a lark's twitter"). I wanted a taut, supple line that imbued a natural American syntax with Pasternak's irrepressible vitality and capacity for regeneration. I decided to translate the poems into free verse, retain Pasternak's stanzas, forego his rhyme and meter, and to parallel his intricate form with a highly stressed, irregular rhythm.

> And so I sang, I sang and died,
> I died and circled back to her
> embraces like a boomerang and—
> as I recall—kept on saying goodbye.
> ("TO LOVE—TO GO—IN ENDLESS THUNDER")

—

I have tried to be clear. But not too clear. For some reason these poems remind me of Keats' letters on the Vale of Soulmaking, the different levels the spirit/imagination has to pass through if it is to grow, and the stress on the necessity that each step be experienced, fully lived, for there to be any movement at all. Pasternak wanted his poems to be steeped in the actual so completely that he wouldn't have to feel indentured to surface reality.

And he was under pressure to do otherwise. Maxim Gorky thought Pasternak's poetry was too elusive and obscure and praised him heartily for simplifying his style and overcoming these "flaws" in *Lieutenant Schmidt*. Gorky meant well. He encouraged Pasternak to be more immediately comprehensible. But it wasn't in Pasternak's character to back off from his perceptions, which rushed into his consciousness, sudden fusions of thoughts and images.

And so we go right up to the pure essence of poetry. It is disturbing, like the ominous turning of a dozen windmills at the edge of a bare field in the black year of famine.

Boris Pasternak, "SOME COMMENTS"

MY SISTER — LIFE

Es braust der Wald, am Himmel zieh'n
Des Sturmes Donnerflüge,
Da mal' ich in die Wetter hin,
O, Mädchen, deine Züge.

Nic. Lenau

IN MEMORY OF THE DEMON

Night after night he came from Tamara's
wrapped in a glacier's blue light.
And marked with his wings
where the nightmare should drone and end.

He did not sob, did not bind
the bare whip-scarred arms.
The gravestone's shadow falls beyond
the fence of the Georgian church.

No matter how wicked the hump
his shadow made no face beneath the lattice.
Next to the icon-lamp the lute
breathed no word of the Princess.

Phosphorous lit through his hair
and the Colossus never heard
how the Caucasus
grieved and went gray.

Two steps from her window
he tugged at the hairs of his cloak,
and whispered into the icy crags: "Sleep, little one,
I'll be an avalanche when I come back!"

ISN'T IT TIME

FOR THE BIRDS TO SING?

ABOUT THESE POEMS

I'll crush them against the pavement
grind them into sun and glass.
I'll shout them at the ceiling
into the cold, moldy corners,

until the winter attic bows,
declaiming to the window panes
as snowdrifts and ragged days
leap like omens in the cornices.

A month long storm will sweep away
the beginning and the end
until, instantly, I'll remember: the sun!
note, the world has changed.

Then Christmas glances like a jackdaw
opening the reckless day
that mystified
my love and me.

Bundled in a muffler, I'll screen
the sun's glare with my palm
and yell to the kids: "Hey,
what millenium is in our yard?"

Who cleared this path to my door,
that hole all choked with snow,
while I was smoking with Byron,
drinking with Poe?

And then I came to Daryal,
that workshop, arsenal, hell,
and with Lermontov's death-quiver on my lips
dipped my life into Vermouth.

LONGING

In the epigraph to this book
deserts go hoarse,
lions roar and Kipling reaches
for a tiger-dawn.

Nostalgia, that black well,
yawns, rolls
them over and they tumble
fur to cold fur.

They tumble through these poems,
fall out of line,
prowl the dew of forests
dreaming of the Ganges.

Dawn, cold, venemous, crawls
into holes. Jungles exhale
the dampness of requiems
and incense.

–:–

My sister—life today floods over
and bursts on everyone in spring rain,
while monocled folk in their grottoes of fine manners
snap and sting, like snakes in oats.

The grownups, of course, have their reasons.
Most likely, most likely your reason's naive,
that eyes and lawns turn violet in the storm
and the horizon smells of moist mignonette;

so that in May, on the Kamyshin branch-line
the schedule of trains you scan in transit
seems grander than the Holy Script,
even though you've read it before;

and only dusk draws swarms
of women crowding onto one platform.
Restless, I hear it's not my stop,
and the sun, setting, takes the seat beside me.

The last bell splashes and floats away
in a prolonged apology: "Sorry ... not yet."
Night smolders under the shutters, and the steppe
stretches from the steps to the stars.

They flicker, blink: my love, a mirage,
and somewhere far away others sleep sweetly
while my heart pours onto every platform
scattering coach doors over the endless plain.

THE WEEPING ORCHARD

It's eerie—how the orchard drips and listens:
  is it the only one in the world
to crumple a branch on this window like lace,
  or is there a witness?

The spongy, bruised earth heaves
  and chokes under the burden.
In the distances you can hear, as in August,
  midnight ripen in the fields.

Not a sound. No one looks on.
  Assured there's no one there
it reverts to old tricks—rolls down roof
  to gutter, and spills over.

I will bring it to my lips and listen:
  am I the only one in the world,
ready to weep on the slightest occasion,
  or is there a witness?

Silence. No breath of leaf, nothing
  in the dark but this weird
gulping, and flapping of slippers,
  and sighs, broken by tears.

THE MIRROR

Steam from a cup of cocoa floods the mirror,
   the sheer curtains stretch and yawn.
Down the straight path, past storms and chaos,
   the mirror runs toward the swings.

There pines toss, impregnating the air
   with resin, and the garden
scatters its eyeglasses in the grass
   where shadows read a book.

Toward the gate, toward dusk in the steppes,
   toward the heady odor of drugged air,
hot quartz shimmers and flows over the road
   laced with snails and branches.

The huge garden wrestles in the room, in the mirror,
   but doesn't break the glass—
as though its collodion flowed above the dresser
   to the noise of tree bark.

The mirrored tide glazes the world
   with sweatless ice, knocking
bitterness into knots, smell into lilacs,
   reigning through mesmerism.

The weird world walks in its sleep,
   and only the wind can bind
what breaks into life, breaks in a prism,
   and gladly plays in tears.

You can't blast the soul with saltpeter
or dig for it, like treasure.
The huge garden wrestles in the room, in the mirror,
    but doesn't break the glass.

In this rich hypnotic country
    you can't blow out my eyes.
And after rain the slugs plug up
    the eyes of garden statues.

Water murmurs in the ears, the pine siskin
    shree and tiptoe daintly.
Go, smear their lips with blueberries,
    they're blind to your mischief.

The huge garden wrestles in the room,
    shakes its fist at the mirror,
runs to the swings, grabs, muddies them,
    but doesn't break the glass!

THE GIRL

A small golden storm slept
on the breast of a giant rock.

Out of the orchard's wildly rocking swings
   a branch bounds into the mirror!
A glistening emerald drop hangs from the end
   of a straight stem.

The orchard hides inside this chaos
   that hits you in the face.
Lovely, large as a orchard, but by nature—
   A sister! Another mirror!

Now you put the branch in a glass
   and set it beside the mirror's frame.
It wonders, who put tears in my eyes
   in this captive human dream?

−:−

You hold that branch in the wind,
test if it's time for the birds to sing,
a branch of wet lilac,
storm-drenched sparrow.

Raindrops—like collar studs—
blind the garden
already fretted
with a million blue tears.

Nurtured by love, its arrows
still in my chest because of her
it sprang back to life
smelling, mumbling.

All night it tapped at the window.
Shutters trembled and
the rancid dampness
sank into your dress.

Stirred out of sleep
by the strange roll call
of ages and names, the day
opens, with eyes like anemones.

RAIN

Inscription on THE BOOK OF THE STEPPE

She's here with me. Play on,
flood, rip the dusk with laughter!
Drown, float, at a tangent
to love, like you, alone!!

Spin, mulberry spindle,
and stampede the windowpane.
Wrap and strap it up,
darken the darkness!

Night at midday, comb of rain.
The sopping rubbish—take it!
And—let the trees shake it
into eyes, temples, and jasmine!

Hail the Egyptian dark!
Raindrops slip and fall and the air
smells as though patients
were released from a thousand hospitals.

It is like the sound of a hundred guitars
plucked in unison,
soaking the lindens in fog
on a hillside of St. Gotthard.

THE BOOK OF THE STEPPE

Est-il possible, – le Fut-il?
Verlaine

BEFORE ALL THIS
THERE WAS THE WINTER

Through lace curtains,
ravens.
In terror of hoarfrost,
omens.

It's the October whirling,
it's terror
crawling, clawing
up the steps.

Sometimes they beg, sometimes they sigh
or groan,
but all rise in unison
for October.

When the wind grabs the trees
by the hands,
it's time to fetch wood
from the cellar.

Snow falls from knees to floor,
entering the store
shouting: "How many winters,
how many years?"

Did the snow so often
trampled
scatter from hooves
like cocaine?

The pain always comes back,
as foam on bits,
in wet salt from clouds, like stains
on a headcloth.

FROM SUPERSTITION

A case with a red orange
    is my den.
I won't go to my grave
    stained by rented rooms.

I settled here the second time
    from superstition.
The wallpaper's brown as oak
    and the door sings.

I wouldn't let go of the doorknob.
    You tried to wriggle free.
My hair touched your forehead,
    my lips touched—violets.

O gentle one, to honor what is gone
    your dress is chirping
like a snowdrop to April:
    "It's good to see you!"

I know you are no virgin, yet
    you entered with a chair,
took my life down from the shelf
    and blew off the dust.

DON'T TOUCH

"Don't touch. Wet paint."
  The soul paid it no mind.
Now memory's stained by calves and cheeks
  and hands and lips and eyes.

More than for any loss or gain
  I loved you because
you caused this white and yellow world
  to turn a whiter white.

My friend, I swear that this dust
  will be whiter than
fever, lampshades, or the white
  bandage on a brow.

–:–

You played that role so well
I forgot I was your prompter,
and that you'll play another part
for others soon.

The boat sailed down the clouds,
down the hayfields.
You played that role so well,
like the stern grazing the sluice-gate.

You hovered at the helm
like a swallow on one wing.
You played that role to the hilt.
Better than anyone.

BALASHOV

Weekdays the cooper hammered,
bent hoops, rounded staves,
and shared a share of oil
with the fire.

Anyway, you were bursting with joy
and the sky chanted, "Take me, I'm yours!"
and poured through the heat,
on wagons and luggage.

The chorale scattered in the rain,
over a grave, on Molokans' caps,
and pine groves hoisted it
to the clouds—that waved goodbye.

Anyway, large as the sun,
Balashov rose and fell,
opening, in early autumn days,
the grief of an old wound.

Drenched in July's blue haze
the marketplace shimmered.
The holy fool, bronchial as a saw,
wheezed through his nose.

My friend, you ask who commands
this fool's babble to burn.
It's in the nature of lindens and graves,
it's in the nature of summer to burn.

THE IMITATORS

It was hot. The riverbank was high.
A chain dropped from the approaching boat
like a rattlesnake onto sand,
like clanging rust onto grass.

Both of them were silhouetted
against the cliff. I wanted to shout:
"Why not throw yourselves separately
or together into the river?"

Your are true to better images.
Clearly, the one who seeks will find.
But quit tormenting your double
here on shore with all your noise!

THE IMAGE

O, poor Homo sapiens,
  it's a rough life.
Only one of your kin
  can pocket the past.

You endure drought and hunger, grow
  savage in war and never get
the point: that the miracle of life
  is the work of an instant.

I drank lilac from her hands,
  whispered to her eyes,
wandered crazed from night to night,
  burning inside.

That southern hut was farther
  south than any other.
Downtrodden, like a stepchild,
  grass wild at its feet.

The canvas has dried. Still,
  after a year has past,
that fence trellised with fox glove
  fills my chest.

O unforgettable year,
  that swelled with dust,
that cracked open sunflower seeds
  and scattered them over burdocks,

that led me blindly
 through nameless mallows,
praying to find you
 behind every gate.

Stepped off the train, threw
 fresh paint on canvas,
sketched a willow grove
 where I found you again.

My train lurches gently
 (still Moscow station),
then wheels and springs jounce over
 bridges and ditches.

Wells hum like kobzas
 in the dust and wind,
haystacks and poplars creak,
 hurling themselves on the earth.

Although life wears out all ties
 and pride warps the mind,
we will die with the pressure
 of what we strive for in our blood.

ENTERTAINMENT FOR

THE BELOVED

−:−

It shakes a fragrant branch,
  drinks its treasure in the dark,
this raindrop, drunk on storm,
  hops from cup to cup.

Rolling from cup to cup,
  it straddles and clings to them,
hangs there like an agate,
  sparkles, and shies away.

Tortured and flattened by wind
  over meadowsweet,
divided, whole—they go on
  drinking, kissing.

Laughing, breaking up again
  then straightening out,
they will never be spilled from the pistils,
  cut them—they will not die.

WITH OARS CROSSED

The rowboat rocks in a drowsy creek.
Dangling willows kiss our wrists,
our elbows, collarbones, oarlocks—but wait,
this could happen to anyone!

This is the drift of song.
This is the lilac's ashes and the splendor
of crushed camomile on dew.
This is to barter lips and lips for stars.

This is to embrace the horizon,
encircle Hercules with your arms.
This is to swirl through time,
squander sleep for nightingales' songs.

SPRING RAINSTORM

It chuckles to a birdcherry and drenches
the laquered carriages, the shivering trees.
Fiddlers wade through the moon's wake
to the theater. Line up, Citizens!

Puddles on cobblestones. Deep roses,
like throats welling with tears,
are sprayed with glistening diamonds.
Whips of joy splash eyelashes and clouds.

First the moon molds the lines,
trembling dresses and enraptured lips;
it molds an epic in plaster,
it molds a bust molded by no one.

In whose heart does the blood rush
toward glory pouring down drawn cheeks?
There the blood beats: the prime minister's hands
strangle aortas and mouths.

It's not the night, not rain, nor the chorus
erupting: "Kerensky, hooray!"
It's a blinding exit to the Forum
from catacombs, that yesterday had no way out.

It's not roses, not mouths, nor the roar
of multitudes thronging at the gates—
but the tide of Europe's night
swelling with pride on our pavements.

POLICEMAN'S WHISTLES

The servants strike. Repelled
by dust and rotting garbage
nights shovel themselves
over the fence.

They scale the forked elms,
lose hold, fall down,
leap: beyond the fence
the North of thievery turns gray.

And from the very orchard
where your eye spent the night,
a flattened whistle
is fished out of the mist.

Frenzied in a cop's fist
it flips its gills,
lifts eyes and throat
with one fishy squint.

The ear-piercing pea
of fibrillating silver pales,
when hurled over the fence
like a gray-blue star.

And to the East where Tivoli
expires in a tubercular summer,
the gutted whistle gasps
clogged by agonizing dust.

THE STARS IN SUMMER

They whisper awful tales,
leave the right address,
open the door, inquire,
shifting places, as on stage.

Silence—you sound better
than anything I've heard.
Some people are annoyed
when bats untuck their wings.

But on July nights,
above the fair-haired settlements,
the sky is flush with mischief
and could play any trick.

Glittering, the stars shower
joy and light
on such and such a latitude
and longitude

The wind lifts a rose
at the request
of lips and hair and shoes
and aprons and nicknames.

Gaseous, hot,
they scatter into the gravel
all that was shuffled,
all that was strummed.

ENGLISH LESSONS

When it was Desdemona's time to sing,
and so little life was left to her,
she wept, not over love, her star,
but over willow, willow, willow.

When it was Desdemona's time to sing
and her murmuring softened the stones
around the black day, her blacker demon
prepared a psalm of weeping streams.

When it was Ophelia's time to sing,
and so little life was left to her,
the dryness of her soul was swept away
like straws from haystacks in a storm.

When it was Ophelia's time to sing,
and the bitterness of tears was more
than she could bear, what trophies
did she hold? Willow, and columbine.

Stepping out of all that grief,
they entered, with faint hearts
the pool of the universe and quenched
their bodies with other worlds.

LECTURES

IN PHILOSOPHY

THE DEFINITION OF POETRY

It's a tightly filled whistle,
it's the squeaking of jostled ice,
it's night, frosting the leaves,
it's two nightingales dueling.

It's the soundlessness of sweetpeas,
the tears of the universe in a pod.
It's a Figaro from music-stands and flutes
like hail on garden plots.

And all that the night finds hard to find
on the sunken floors of bathhouses
is carried to the fish pond
like a star on damp, trembling palms.

It's mugginess flatter than sunken boards,
alders banked over the horizon.
The laughter of the stars is welcome
in this universe—soundless place.

THE DEFINITION OF SOUL

It falls like a ripe pear into the storm
with a single clinging leaf.
How faithful—it quits its branch—
reckless—it chokes in the heat.

It falls like a pear, more askew
than the wind. How faithful—
Look back: it thundered beautifully,
bloomed, scattered—into ashes.

The storm burned our country.
Fledgling, will you know your nest?
O my quivering goldfinch, my leaf,
why do you flutter against my shy silk?

Do not fear, my single clinging song.
What should we strive for?
O indivisible trembling—you don't get
that deadly phrase "stay put."

DISEASES OF EARTH

More! When laughter erupts
with mother of pearl, bacterial tides,
wet rumblings and staphylococcus clouds,
knives will flash like lightning.

Then—enough! Immovable titans
will choke in the black vaults of day.
Then tetanus will retrieve the shadows,
and snakes go into torpor.

The flood is here! Glitter of watery fear,
wind, shards of vicious spitting.
Where? From clouds, from fields, from Kliazma,
or from one sardonic pine?

Are these poems fermented
enough to stun the thunder?
It must have been delirious
to consent to be the earth.

THE DEFINITION OF ART

Tearing open its shirt, to expose
Beethoven's hirsute torso,
it places its palms, like checkers, over
sleep and conscience, night and love.

And with what dark longing,
wild grief and havoc,
it conjures the world's end
on horseback over pawns on foot.

The root cellar's ice is rife
with the *oohs* and *aahs* of stars.
Cool Tristan, full-throated, gasps,
like a nightingale over Isolde's vine.

And gardens, and ponds, and fences,
and the fever of creation,
release the desire
stored up in the spirit.

THE THUNDERSTORM

The storm, like a priest, burned the lilac,
and veiled eyes and clouds
with sacrificial smoke. Go,
mend the ant's sprained leg with your lips.

Pealing of toppled pails.
What greed: Isn't the sky enough?!
A hundred hearts beat in the ditch.
The storm burned the lilac, like a priest.

Brittle gleam on the meadow; azure
earth dimmed by frost and ice;
finches in no hurry to shake
the crystal haze from their souls.

They still drink the storm from barrels,
overflowing with fresh water;
clover darkens, a burgundy hue
under the brushy thunder clouds.

Mosquitoes stick to raspberries.
That vicious malarial proboscis
thrusts itself—the pagan—
where summer's rosiest,

injects an abscess through a blouse,
pirouettes like a red ballerina
and jabs its stinger of mischief
where blood clots like wet leaves.

O, believe my game, and believe
that migraine raging at your heels!
The wrathful day burns
in the bark of wild cherry trees.

Do you believe? Then lean your cheek
a little nearer, nearer still,
and in the dawn of your holy summer
my breath will fan it into flame.

I won't keep secrets from you,
who hide your lips in jasmine snow.
I feel that snow on my lips too:
it melts on mine in sleep.

What can I do with my joy?
Put it in poems? Ruled notebooks?
Its lips are already parched from poisons
on written sheets.

At war with the alphabet,
they burn as blushes on your cheeks.

These diversions ceased when, as she was leaving,
she passed her mission on to her substitute,
the one who took her place.

THE SUBSTITUTE

—:—

I live with your photograph, the one with your shy laughter,
where wrist joints snap,
where knuckles crack but don't fall off,
and the guests feast and grieve.

It runs from the crackling logs, from the bravado of Liszt,
from the chandelier in the ballroom, from glasses and guests,
over the piano in flames and jumps—
from rosettes and dice, roses and knucklebones.

Your hair ruffled, high on tea,
and with that fragrant bud pinned to your sash,
you waltz into the sunset, gesturing like an idiot,
biting your scarf as if in pain.

Crumbling tangerine rinds in your fingers,
you gulp down the cool cool wedges,
then sweep into the mirrored hall
and the perspiration of waltzes.

This is how the gale subsides
on a blind bet,
enduring thorns like a Moslem monk
without blinking.

And declares that not a horse,
not the wild murmuring of mountains,
but only roses on a slope
gallop over you.

Not it, not the murmuring mountains,
not it, not the clopping hooves,
but only that, but only that—
what's huddled in a shawl.

But only that, which runs like lace,
soul, or sash, to the rhythm
of whirlwinds and the tip of her runaway shoe
escapes upstream in dreams.

To them, to them—
laughing them off their feet,
to the envy of running sacks,
to tears—to tears!

SONGS IN LETTERS

THAT SHE WOULD NOT BE LONELY

SPARROW HILLS

My kisses, like water from a pitcher,
pour over your breast. Summer is not endless.
Not, night after night, will we raise the dust,
stomp to the low bellow of accordions.

I've heard of old age—such blighted forecasts.
When no wave will raise its arms toward the stars.
They say—to deaf ears—there is no face in the meadows,
no heart in the rivers, no god in the groves.

Get your soul in motion, stretch it like a sail!
It's the world's midday—open your eyes!
Can you see, in the heights, thoughts simmer in the white foam
of woodpeckers, fir cones, clouds, pine needles, and heat.

This is where the rails for city trolleys end.
Beyond, pines hold sermons. Beyond, rails can't stretch.
Beyond that, it's Sunday. Snapping branches
the clearing scampers downhill, sliding on the grass.

Sifting the midday of Whitsuntide, and romping,
the grove begs, "Believe me—it's always like this."
It's divined by thickets, prophesied to clearings,
and sprinkled on our cotton by the clouds.

MEIN LIEBCHEN, WAS WILLST DU NOCH MEHR?

Arrows scramble down the wall.
Time crawls like a cockroach.
Wait, why toss the plates,
beat the alarm, smash the glasses!

In our wooden dacha
anything could happen
Lightning didn't strike—
so why cross yourself?

It might have hit and flickered
in the damp cabin, the puppies
might have been abandoned,
or rain buckshot the wing.

The forest is our backyard,
the spruce-bound moon our stove.
Drying, the storm mumbles,
like a freshly washed apron.

And when grief's whirlwind
storms the well, and thunder
claps for domesticity—
what else could you want?

The year guttered in kerosene
like a gnat trapped in a lamp,
then got up, a gray-blue star,
sleepy and wet.

Old, tremulous, fretful,
it peeks into the window's parenthesis,
moistening the pillow
where it buried its tears.

How can we cheer up that grump
who has no sense of humor,
how can we quench the unheard
sorrow of abandoned summer?

The forest is draped in lead,
the gray burdocks frown,
but you're amazing, like the day,
and rest in fitfulness.

Why is that old grump crying?
Did it glimpse another's joy?
Do village sunflowers sulk
in the dust and rain?

RASPAD

> Again you could see far,
> to all ends of the world.
> *Gogol*

How can we mark time?
How can we shed rot, Raspad?
On the Volga coast, sleepless,
unleashed miracles clamor.

Where the eye relied
on the droughty steppe for mercy,
there, in swirling mist,
the haystack of revolution rises.

In distant granaries and silos
rats get drunk on wheat,
beams and stacks catch fire,
rooftops settle like dew.

Puzzled stars hold hot, silent disputes:
Where did Balashov disappear?
Is Khoper the nearest river?
The air of the steppe is alerted.

It senses, it drinks the spirit
of soldiers' riots and heat lightning,
halts, turns into ears,
lies down, hears: "Turn around."

Hollow rumblings. Can't sleep.
Tinder flickers across the square.
There, night shakes on its root
and kisses the coal of dawn.

That summer they went there from
Paveletsky Station.

ROMANOVKA

THE STEPPE

How lovely those walks into silence!
The steppe wide and quiet, like a bay.
Feathergrass sighs. Ants shimmer.
And mosquitoes wail.

Haystacks and clouds form a row
darkening the singed ochre volcanoes.
The steppe, hushed and wet, goes on
rocking, nudging, pushing,

Haystack in mist? Who can tell?
Is it a tent? Closer, closer: yes!
Found it at last! Our very own tent.
The steppe and fog on all four sides.

Fog walls us in on all four sides.
Thistles clutch and tug at our socks.
It's eerie to wade across this steppe
rocked, nudged, and pushed.

The Milky Way lays a path to Kerch,
like a dusty cattletrodden road.
Step out—it takes your breath away—
space—open—all four sides!

Feathergrass, honey, reveries, fog.
Feathergrass scattered over the Milky Way.
The fog lifts, and darkness surrounds
the tent and steppe on all four sides.

Midnight stands darkly on the road,
and burdened by stars, tumbles down.
You can't step beyond your fence
without trampling the universe.

When did stars grow so close to the ground,
and midnight dive into weeds,
and sopping muslin shiver,
clinging, cuddling, craving the end?

Let the steppe judge. Let the night forgive,
when and when not: In the Beginning
The Wailing of Mosquitoes, Rustling of Ants,
And Thistles Clutching at Socks.

Close the tent, love! There's too much dust!
The steppe's as pure as before the Fall:
wrapped in the universe like a parachute,
like an apparition, rising.

A SULTRY NIGHT

It drizzled, but didn't bend
the grass in the storm's sack.
Dust swallowed pills of rain,
iron in a quiet powder.

The village was past healing.
Even a deep poppy swooned.
Rye flared with St. Anthony's fire
and God trudged, delirious.

In the orphaned, sleepless,
damp universal waste,
groans tore from their posts,
the whirlwind dug in, abated.

Drops squinted in blind pursuit.
Pale wind and wet branches
bickered at the fence. I held my
breath: they fought over me!

I felt that this garrulous garden
could babble into eternity.
When I'm off the street, beyond
the speech of shrubs and shutters—I'll be safe.
Once they spot me—no way out:
they'll talk, talk, talk me to death!

AN EVEN MORE SULTRY DAWN

All morning a dove cooed
at your window.
Branches
sprawled in the gutters
like wet sleeves.
Fine rain. Clouds, raggedly dressed,
crossed the dusty market,
rocking,
I'm afraid,
my longing on a market stall.
I pleaded with them to stop.
They seemed to stop.
Gray dawn, like the quarreling of bushes,
like prisoners' talk.

I pleaded for that time
when beyond your window
the washbasin would roar
like an avalanche
and the kindled bits of your song
and the heat of your sleepy cheeks and forehead
would pour like ice
into the glass on your dresser.

But the sky, under the banners
of mumbling clouds,
did not hear my prayer
through the heavy silence,

sodden, like an army overcoat,
like the dusty sound of threshing,
like a noisome squabble in the bushes.
I pleaded with them—
don't torture me!
I can't sleep!

But it went on drizzling,
and clouds kept crossing the dusty market
like recruits filing past a farmhouse at dawn,
not for an hour, not for a century,
like Austrian prisoners of war,
like a muffled gasp,
like a hoarse cry:
"Sister ...
some ... water ...."

THE ATTEMPT TO

SEPARATE THE SOUL

MOOCHKAP

The spirit sweats—the horizon's
tobacco-tinged—like thought.
Windmills image a fishing village:
boats and weathered nets.

The village of torpid windmills
hovers like a motionless harbor.
All smells of weary stasis,
uneasiness, and grief.

The hours skip past like stones,
richochet across the shallows,
not drowning, keeping afloat,
tobacco-tinged—like thought.

There's time before the train
but it's drowned by apathy,
sunk in limbo, the roiling
turbulence before a storm.

THE FLIES OF THE MOOCHKAP
TEAHOUSE

If a frown is carved
on your sweaty forehead,
does that make me a criminal?
Do I have to get out now?

But in the teahouse, where black cherries
peer out of eye sockets and bowls
at the bridal shower of branches,
now, that's reason to wonder!

The sun's like blood on a knife,
washed—it gives off a strange glow.
That's to say, black tea floods the room
in the heat of transgression.

A poppy wilts in the dust,
each petal thirsting
for the coolness of God's
wild, bitter thickets.

You call me Saint.
If I'm so focused and intense,
what about the painted flowers
on the clock and china?

It's still unknown
on which page of earth's sphere
a river of heat is imprinted,
and barking of sheepdogs,

an oak, and enameled billboards,
sun-crazed, collapse
and hurl themselves
into the jaspered pond.

But even after dark, flies flow
by the dozen from steaming portions,
from the "twisted lord"
and the poet's muddy book.

It's as though some delirious pen
had squirted out of control,
like locusts blotting the windows,
crowding the wallpaper.

It's as though the time had come
for all springs to leap from their hinges,
for the whirring spiral of storm
to spin around the poplar.

But where, in what place,
in what country of wild thoughts?
I know drought and thunder, and when
a storm will break in July—I know.

–:–

What a wild party, and wild ride home.
I could hardly drag my legs.
How your cheeks puffed with rage
as you glued your eyes to the wall.

Your hostile silence backfired:
it only fueled my longing.
If your lips are locked in silence
why not also lock the door.

No, don't, don't lock the door
while denial hangs on your heart.
You and you alone lend
some clarity to my life.

If I'd known I would have to drag
a crossbeam over my head
or press my eyes against your eyes,
swollen from distress,

I would have run known to the earth,
and seen at the road's end
the spotted sun under lock
and the rot of captive springtime.

Don't let my soul be riddled
by deceit: kill it or,
like fog, it will seep through
a heap of white chaff.

If, on a sultry afternoon,
the yellow corn kilns reek of mice,
assure me it's the false
witnessing of love that lies.

-:-

We have tried to separate our souls
but the names Moochkap and Rzhaksa,
like the wailing of violins,
strike deep chords of grief.

I love those names as I love you,
as if they were you.
Vainly, and in vain, I love you.
I'm losing my wits!

Like a night that shadows the stars,
like muslin riven by asthma,
as you bare your shoulders
the staircase quivers.

Whose hesitant whisper is that?
Mine? No. It must be yours.
It flew from your lips
like aery drops of spirits.

A thought cleared in the calm.
Irreproachable. Like a groan.
Like a headland, suddenly at midnight,
illuminated on all three sides.

THE RETURN

–:–

How life lulls us—how all
is revealed to the sleepless!
Can you sunder your grief
on the foundations of bridges?

Where the smoky semaphore
chased night off the tracks:
where the bridge of the Apocalypse
rocks the sighs of stars,
where beams, ribs, rails, and ties
gather in a shrieking avalanche,

where jostled bodies grasp
hands, break embraces,
chant and repeat
a tireless refrain,

where the dipstick thrusts
benzine into faces
clinging like soot
on the ends of dead cigars ...

It's a burning tulip,
wild begonia fire,
inhaled by the crowd
through cupped palms.

The delicate pistils
burn as if ashamed,

every fifth one—engineer,
student, "intelligensia."

I am not one of them.
I was sent by God to torment
myself, my family, everyone
whom it's a sin to torment.

Near Kiev—sand
and splattered tea
stick to hot foreheads,
in fever—by social class.

Near Kiev—sand
in multitudes, like boiling water,
like the freshly washed trace
of a compress, like dropsy ...

The tall pines can't dilute
this puffing, soot, and heat—
and now the storm juts out
of the forest like an ax!

But the woodcutter, where is he?
How long will all this last?
Which road leads to the depot?

Passengers clamber aboard,
the bell rings, the whistle hoots,
and the smoke spawns
a desert of its own.

Bazaars, illuminations
of night's finery, fog,
the laments of noon and a saw
burst through the roadside weeds.

You stretch your legs, hear
sobbing in the sheds—
hens and mattress springs
clucking, coupling in the sun.

I am not one of them.
I was sent by God to torment
myself, my family, everyone
whom it's a sin to torment.

Coffee, cigarettes, kefir.
It takes so little
to make me burst into tears—
some flies on a windowpane will do.

The pig in horseradish
sends tears down my napkin,
blurring my field of vision
like yawning rye.

For me to burst into tears
it takes only the odor
of tobacco from an editor's door,
or heat to descend

or the click click of an abacus
amidst office gossip,

or desperate clouds to blow out
their brains on cucumbers,

or for high noon to strike
through the gauze of sleep,
or empty tables to rattle
at the call of cafés,

or the shadow of a raspberry bush
cooling my sweating forehead,
where greenhouses glimmer,
where the white body of a clinic stands.

I am not one of them.
I was sent by God to torment
myself, my family, everyone
whom it's a sin to torment.

Can it be that this midday moment
in a southern province
is not wet, barefoot, or hungry,
but racked with ecstasy?

Does that sulky, superfluous,
railroad hobo, that leech,
spy an angel's embroidery
on neighboring cherry trees?

Suddenly noon turns blue
as a sea of dots, and stoops
like a boneless shadow
hurled upon tired shirts.

Can it be that those willows—
chased away by railroad ties—
hurl themselves in a giddy spasm
toward some miraculous embrace?

Will they come back at night,
breathe essence from a wing
and start to play the housewife
over the strife of towels?

Will they spot the hazel's shadow
on a stone foundation,
or trace the spent day
in smoldering dusk?

Why make distress persist,
sifting through trivia?
The watchman switches our memory,
and chases us off the tracks.

AT HOME

Heat wavers over the seven hills,
doves cluck on the mildewed hay.
The sun removes its turban:
time to change the towel
(soaking in the pit of the pail)
then wrap it around my cupola.

In town—gossip of vocal cords,
jumbled flowerbeds and dolls.
Quick, stitch the curtains:
it's strutting like a Mason.
How life lulls us to sleep!
How rapture wracks our nights!

Grimy, groaning, the city streets
tumble into bed.
Today, at last, the steppe releases
a healing breeze.
No way to exhaust all the curses,
the sultry, black names for heat.
Stars, posters, bridges,
go to sleep!

They left from Pavelestky that fall too.

TO HELEN

TO HELEN

I wouldn't censor
an unprintable word,
but on whom can we find one?
On no one, from no one.

Does arum ever ask for
charity from the marsh?
Nights are free to inhale
this thick, tropical stench.

This hope—this endless longing
for you to be here, for an age,
lily-like and young forever,
drives me mad!

The field adopted a habit
of Hamlet, no, of Faust,
and paced, like the daisy,
ankle-high in stalks.

Or, in half sleep, dimly
flickering, visible, invisible,
a cluster of pearls
on Ophelia's neck.

The farmhouse had bad dreams;
plumed clouds disturbed
its sleep and rain wrapped
the fields in the quiet

threads of assiduous drops.
Youth swam in bliss, like
a sleepy pillow under
a child's night-breath.

I hope Troy thrived when it kissed
her bitter twisted lips:
those were the great ages,
kingly, capped in gypsum.

Dear, deathly apron,
dear pulsating temple,
sleep, Queen of Sparta,
it's still early, still damp.

Grief wasn't joking when it began
to clown with your life.
You ought to be scared to face it alone.
If it raves, can you handle it?

Cry, it whispered, does it gnaw?
Does it burn? One more on her cheek!
Let fate decide if she was
mother or stepmother.

AS WITH THEM

The face of azure beams above the face
of this breath-taking, beloved river.
A catfish surfaces. A sudden splash.
Deafening. Far off. Echoing.

It's hard on eyes sheaved like eaves,
two hearths glowing with embers.
The face of azure beams above the forehead
of the breath-taking lady of the deep,
of the breath-taking stepchild of the sedge.

The wind lifts alfalfa laughter,
blows kisses down the valley,
gorges on marshberries, crawls,
smears its lips with ferns, tickles
the river's cheek with a branch
or sours and ferments in the reeds.

Will a sunfish fan its fins?
The day is swollen, deep and red.
The river's tray is black lead:
can't tie the ends or raise my hand ...

The face of azure beams above the face
of this breath-taking, beloved river.

SUMMER

It brought an entourage of thirst,
stingers, butterflies, and stains,
weaving tapestries from its memory
of mayflower, mint, and honey.

Not the ticking of clocks
but the day-long jangle of chains
pierced the air with drowsy thorns
and cast a spell on the weather.

It happened—the sunset,
tired of games, passed
dominion over the kitchen garden
to cicadas, stars, and trees.

The moon shed beams, not shadows,
and disappeared without a sound,
while quietly the night rippled
from cloud to cloud.

More from dreams than from eaves,
more absent minded than timid,
the light rain shuffled at the door
and smelled of wine-cork.

That's how the dust smelled. And the weeds.
And once you got the point,
that's how the gentry's decrees smelled:
of brotherhood, equality.

They installed councils in the provinces.
Did you, friend, cast your lot with them?
Days glittered in the sorrel,
and smelled of wine-cork.

STORM, AN ENDLESS INSTANT

Summer waved goodbye to the wayside
station. Then thunder
took off its cap and snapped
a hundred blinding photographs.

A lilac cluster dimmed and
thunder gathered sheaves
of lightning to expose, from far
fields, the overseer's house.

And waves of terror, malevolent,
lashed and crackled on the roof,
and a stockade of rain fell
like charcoal strokes on paper.

Deep in the brain something blinked:
it felt as though those corners
of the mind would burst into light
where it's already bright as day.

—:—

They will extract a price, my love. The gods
grow too enamoured of this "poetic" love.
And raw chaos crawls out of the cave,
toward original light.

The tons of fog that pour from his eyes,
fur him in fog like a mammoth.
He may be out of fashion—but knows:
ages pass—the world's still illiterate.

He sees how they make merry at weddings:
getting drunk, passing out, sleeping
it off; or how they call some frogspawn,
plumped on a silver plate, "Beluga."

How life, like a pearly jest
out of Watteau, they would
snuff out in snuff boxes;
while they twist, mangle, and distort,

while they lie and flatter and smile,
while they rut in heat like drones,
he lifts your sister up, like a baccante
on an urn, and takes her.

He pours the Andes' thaw in his kiss,
pours dawn under the dust of stars
when night huddles in villages
that fill with white fleecy "baas."

And he inhales the breath of ancient ravines,
the dark botanic sacristy,
smells typhus in a mattress
and spurts through the chaos of thickets.

–:–

My friend, you ask who commands
that this holy fool's babble should burn.

Let the words drop like amber
or zest in orchards,
thoughtless and abundant,
again, again, again.

There is no need to explain
why the leaves are
so ceremoniously sprayed
with lemon and madder.

Who made pine needles
shed tears and jet
through railings and screens
to land on music stands.

Who blackened the doormat
with beads of mountain ash
shimmering like a quilt
of transparent italics.

You ask who commands
August to be august,
to whom nothing is trivial,
who dwells in the last

vanishings of maple leaves
and stands by his post
during the hewing of alabaster
since Ecclesiastes?

You ask who commands
the lips of September's
asters and dahlias to suffer,
or spines of golden broom
to fall off gray caryatids
onto the dank gravestones
of autumn hospitals?

You ask who commands?
Almighty God of detail,
Almighty God of lovers,
of Yagailos and Yadvigas.

I don't know if they've solved
the riddle of the dark beyond the grave,
but life is like this silence:
autumnal, particular.

THERE WERE

Afterwards, there were windrows
and the odor of wine-cork.
When August ran out of days,
weeds took over the path.

In the grass and in the sorrel
sullen diamonds clung
and tasted so frosty
they reminded us of Riesling.

September wrote the program
for carts at harvest time,
ran, conducted, and foretold
of bad weather ahead.

Or shaded the yard with wine and water,
yellowed the sand and puddles,
or sprinkled lead down from the sky
onto dormer windows.

Or burnished them, wheeling
over a bush—to barns and peasants,
or pelted the windowpane
with raging, fiery leaves.

There are signs of joy, words,
vin gai, vin triste—believe me—
grass is grass, sorrel is sorrel,
and Riesling, a dusty name.

There were nights. There used to be
trembling lips. Sullen diamonds
on eyelids. Rain roared in the brain,
not bursting into thought.

Maybe I don't really love—I pray
when lovers kiss. The mollusc,
not for an hour, not for eternity,
floats by in joyful light.

Like music: the ages weep,
but song isn't born to cry,
quivering, a coraline softness,
not bursting into "ah!"

–:–

To love—to go—in endless thunder,
to stamp out grief, wear no shoes,
to spook hedgehogs, to pay good
for evil to cranberries in cobwebs.

To drink from branches that whip your face,
snap back and slash the azure:
"So that's an echo!"—and in the end
to lose your way in her kisses.

To ramble through a landscape of turnips!
To know at sunset that the sun
is older than those stars and carts,
older than Margarita and the Innkeeper.

To lose your tongue like a subscription
to a storm of tears in Valkyries' eyes,
to grow as numb as the sweltering sky,
to drown the forest masts in ether.

Stretched out in thorns, rake up
the residue of years like pinecones:
on the highway; Sign of an Inn;
dawn; frozen; eating fish.

And lying down, to sing again:
"Old and gray, I walked and fell.
The town was choked with weeds
washed by the tears of soldiers' wives.

In the shadow of a moonless barn,
in the flames of flagons and groceries,
this old, worn out husk of a man
will perish in his time."

And so I sang, I sang and died.
I died and circled back to her
embraces like a boomerang and—
as I remember—kept on saying goodbye.

POSTSCRIPT

No, I wasn't the source of your grief.
I didn't beg my country's oblivion.
The sun burned on drops of ink
like clusters of dusty currants.

Cochineal spread through the blood
of every thought I had and word I wrote.
I didn't cause that wormy redness.
No, I wasn't the source of your grief.

It was the evening molded out of the dust
that kissed you, choking in ochre pollen.
It was shadows taking your pulse; it was you
turning your face toward the fields
that burned, swimming on the hinges of gates
flooded with dusk, ashes and poppies.

It was the whole summer in a blaze of pods
and labels and sun-bleached luggage
sealing the wanderer's breast with wax,
setting your hats and dresses on fire.

It was your eyelashes glued by the sun,
it was that savage disk butting its horns
against walls, flattening fences.
It was the carbuncular sunset humming in your hair,
perishing there for half an hour,
shaking the purple off marigolds and raspberries.
No, it wasn't my love, but your loveliness.

THE END

Is it all real? Is it time now to drift away?
No—better to sleep, sleep, sleep, sleep,
and see no dreams.

Another street. Another night. Another canopy of tulle.
Once again—steppe, haystack, groan,
now and forever.

Wheezing in every atom the August leaves
dream of darkness and silence. The sound of the dog's
big paws awakens the orchard.

It waits—they'll settle down. A giant grows out
of the dark … then another. Footsteps. "Here's the bolt!"
Whistles: got it!

It literally drowned the road with our footsteps,
brought it all the way down and racked the fence
with images of you.

Autumn. The threading of gray-blue and yellow beads.
Decay, I long for oblivion. Like you I am sick
to death of living.

O and now is the worst time for trains to shuttle past,
switch tracks and wait, now, when in the rain each leaf
surges toward the steppe!

Windows frame senseless scenes. And to what end?!
To let the door spring from its hinges having kissed
the ice on her elbows?

Make known to me someone who's been reared, as they have been,
on the hard road at the end of southern harvests,
waste land and rye.

But with the bitter aftertaste, numbness, cold, and lumps
in the throat, but with the sorrow of so many words
you bring this friendship to an end.

THE HIGHEST SICKNESS

The shifting riddle glitters,
the siege goes on, days go on,
the months and years go by.
One lovely day, the messengers,
panting and falling off their feet,
came bearing news: the fort had fallen.
They believe and don't believe, set fires,
blow up the vaults, seek the points of entry,
they come and go—the days go by.
The months and years go by.
The years go by—in shadow.
It's the rebirth of the Trojan epic.
They believe and don't believe, set fires,
agitate and wait for the break;
they falter, go blind—the days go by—
and the walls of the fort fall apart.

I grow more and more ashamed each day
that in an age of shadows
the highest sickness escapes censure
and still goes by the name of song.
Is Sodom the proper name for song
learned by ear the hard way,
then hurled out of books
only to be skewered by spears and bayonets?
Hell is paved with good intentions.
The current notion is
that by paving your poems with them
your sins will be forgiven.
Such gossip rips the ears of silence
on its way back from the war,

and these devastating days have shown
how taut our hearing is strung.

In those turbulent days everyone
was infected with a passion for rumors,
and lice made winter twitch
like the ears of spooked horses,
and all night snowy ears
rustled quietly in darkness
while we tossed fairy tales back and forth,
sprawled on peppermint cushions.

In Spring the upholstery
of theater boxes was seized with trembling.
Poverty-stricken February
groaned, coughed blood,
and tiptoed off to whisper
into the ears of boxcars
about this and that,
railroad ties and tracks,
the thaw, and babbled on, of troops
foot-slogging home from the front.
You sleep, waiting for death,
but the narrator doesn't care.
In the ladles of thawed galoshes
the cloth lice will swallow the lie
tied to the truth without
ceasing to twitch their ears.

Although the dawn thistle
kept on chasing its shadow
and in the same motion
made the hour linger;
although, as before, the dirt road

dragged the wheels over soft white sand
and spun them onto harder ground
alongside signs and landmarks;
although the autumn sky was cloudy,
and the forest appeared distant,
and the twilight was cold and hazy;
anyway, it was all a forgery.
And the sleep of the stunned earth
was convulsive, like labor pains,
like death, like the silence
of cemeteries, like that unique quiet
that blankets the horizon,
shudders, and beats its brains
to remember: Hold on, prompt me,
what did I want to say?

Although, as before, the ceiling,
installed to support a new cell,
lugged the second story to the third
and dragged the fifth to the sixth
suggesting by this shift that everything
was as it used to be—
and anyway, it was all a forgery;
and through the network of waterpipes
rushed the hollow reverberation
of a dark age; the stench
of laurel and soybean,
smoldering in the flames of newspapers
even more indigestible than these lines,
rises into air like a pillar
as though muttering to itself: Hold on, prompt me,
what did I want to eat?

And crept like a famished tapeworm

from the second floor to the third,
and stole from the fifth to the sixth.
It gloried in callousness and regression,
declared tenderness illegal.
What could be done? All sound
drowned in the roar of torn skies.
The roar passed the railroad platform,
vanished beyond the water tower
and drifted to the end of the forest,
where the hills broke out in rashes,
where snowdrifts
pumped through the pines,
and the blinded tracks itched
and rubbed against the blizzard.

And against the backdrop of blazing legends,
the idiot, the hero, the intellectual
burned in decrees and posters
for the glory of a dark force,
that carried them with a grin
around blind corners, if not
for heroic acts, then because two and two
won't add up to a hundred in a day.
And at the rear of blazing legends,
the idealist-intellectuals
wrote and printed posters
on the joys of their twilight.

Huddled in sheepskin, the serf
looked back at the darkening north
where snow gave all it had
to ward off death by twilight.
The railroad station glistened
like a pipe organ in mirrored ice,

and groaned with opened eyes.
And its wild beauty quarreled
with an empty Conservatory
shut down for holiday repairs.
The insidiously silent typhus
gripped our knees, and dreamt

and shuddered as he listened
and heard the stagnant gushing
of monotonous remorse.
The typhus knew all the gaps in the organ
and gathered dust in the seams
of the bellows' burlap shirts.
His well-tuned ears implored
the fog, the ice, and the puddles
splattered over the earth
to keep their silence out of the rain.

We were the music of ice.
I mean my own crowd—we pledged
to quit this stage together,
and I will quit—someday.
There is no room left for shame.
I wasn't put on this earth
to gaze three ways into men's eyes.
More insidious than this song
is the double-crossing word "enemy."
I am a guest and—all over the world—
This is the Highest Sickness:
I wanted to be like everyone else,
but our earth-shaking age
is stronger than my grief
and tries to mimic me.

We were the music of cups,
gone to sip tea in the dark
of deaf forests, oblique habits,
and secrets flattering to no one.
Frosts crackled. Pails hung.
Jackdaws soared and the frost-bitten year
was ashamed to show up at the gates.
We were the music of thought
and sought to sweep the stairs,
but as the cold froze,
ice blurred the passage.

Yet I witnessed the Ninth Congress
of the Soviets and, in the raw twilights,
ran from place to place in the city,
cursing life, cursing the cobblestones
and on the second day, the fabled
day of celebration, went
to the theater in a frantic mood
with a pass to the orchestra pit.
My feet moved soberly on somber rails.
I glanced around: the entire countryside
was a smoldering ash-heap,
stubbornly refusing to rise
off the railway ties.
The Karelian question stared
from every poster, and raised
the question in the eyes of anemic birches.
Thick snow ribboned the crossbars
of telegraph poles and in the fabric
of branches the winter day was shutting down,
not of its own accord, but in response
to a command. At that instant,
like a moral in a fairy tale,

the story of The Congress was revealed:
telling again how the fever of genius
is stronger and whiter than cement.
(Whoever didn't help push that pushcart
should suffer it in the future.)
How all at once, within a week,
the walls of a Citadel arose
in the blinded eyes of the creator,
or at least a dwarfish fort.

The new feeds the rows of ages,
yet its golden pie, wolfed down
before tradition can steep the sauce,
sticks in your throat.
Now, from a certain distance
the trivial details blur,
the stereotypical speeches are forgotten.
Time levels the details
where trivia once prevailed.

The farce was not prescribed
to cure my impatient nature.
And yet I have no memory of how
the voting went so smoothly.
I've managed to exorcise that day,
when, from the bottom of the sea,
through a yawning Japanese abyss,
a telegram was able to distinguish
(what a scholarly deep sea diver!)
classes of octopi frm the working classes.
But those firebreathing mountains
were beyond the range of its concern.
There were countless dumber things to do
than classifying Pompeii.

For a long time I knew by heart
that scandalous telegram
we sent the victims of the tragedy
to soften the roar of Fujiyama
with more pablum from our Trade Unions.

Wake up, poet, show your pass.
You can't yawn at a time like this.
Msta, Ladoga, Sheksna, Lovat.
Leap from box seats over the chairs into the pit.
Once again from Proclamation Hall,
through the door that opened southward,
Peter the Great's arctic blizzard
fanned past the lamps.
Again the frigate went broadside.
Again gulping tidal waves
the child of treason and deceit
doesn't recognize its country.
The earth drowsed, when, running out
from under the Czar's train
with a wild shout,
hunters' packs scattered over the ice.
Tradition hid its stature
behind the railroad structure,
under the railroad bridge.
The pullman cars and the veiled
two-headed eagles lingered
in a black field where the earth
heaved with the odor of March.
At Porkovo, a watery tarpaulin
billowed for a hundred nautical miles;
the gunpowder factory yawned
over the long Baltic shore.

And the two-headed eagle slowed down,
and circled the Pskov region
where the ring of anonymous rebellion
was tightening.
If only they could find a road
not marked on maps!
But the stock of railroad ties
checked on maps was melting fast.
Still meticulous in crisis
they stoked with only the choicest cloth.
Streams frolicked along the tracks;
the future sank in the mud.
The circle shrank, the pines thinned out—
two suns met in the window:
one rising over Tosno;
the other sinking over Dno.

How should I finish my fragment?
I remember his turn of phrase
that struck at me with a white flame
like a whiplash of lightning bolts.
The audience rose and with squinting eyes,
scanned the far table
when he grew onto the platform,
grew before he reached the stage.
He slithered invisibly
through rows of obstacles
like a ball of storm
bolting into a smokeless room.

The roar of ovations broke over us
like relief, like the explosion
of a nucleus that has to explode
in a ring of hurdles and supports.

He opened his mouth. "We are here
to remember . . . the monuments . . . of the fallen . . .
I talk . . . of transitory things. . . . " What in that moment
came to exemplify only him?

He was—like the thrust of a rapier.
Chasing the stream of his talk
he thumbed his vest, planted his heel,
and hammered his point home.
He could have been talking about axle grease
but the taut bow of his body
excluded that naked essence
which tore through the layers of husks.
His naked guttural tones
punctured our ears with truths
implied by the blood of fables:
he was their sound reflection.
Envious with the envy of ages,
jealous with their singular jealousy,
he lorded over their thoughts
and because of that—over their country.

When I saw him there on the stage
I dwelled endlessly, to no end,
on his authority and right
to strive from the first person.

From the rows of generations
someone steps to the front,
bearing the promise of thaws,
and revenges his departure with terror.